Poke the Box

THE
DOMINO
PROJECT

POWERED BY
amazon.com

POKE
THE
BOX

When was the last time

you did something for

the first time?

By Seth Godin

The Domino Project

© 2011 by Do You Zoom, Inc.

The Domino Project

Published by Do You Zoom, Inc.

The Domino Project is powered by Amazon. Sign up for updates and free stuff at www.thedominoproject.com

This is the first edition. If you'd like to suggest a riff for a future edition, please visit our website.

LIBRARY OF CONGRESS CATALOGING IN PUBLICATION DATA

Godin, Seth, 1960—

Poke the Box: When was the last time you did something for the first time? / Seth Godin

p. cm.

ISBN 978-1-936719-00-6

Printed in the United States of America

POKE THE BOX

The job isn't to catch up to the status quo;

the job is to invent the status quo.

The initiator

Annie Downs works at the Mocha Club, a nonprofit based in Nashville that raises money for the developing world by working with touring musicians.

Last year, she called her boss and said something she had never said before. "I've got an idea, and I'm going to start working on it tomorrow. It won't take a lot of time and it won't cost a lot of money, and I think it's going to work."

With those two sentences, Annie changed her life. And she changed her organization and the people it serves.

You're probably wondering what her idea was. You might even be curious about how she pulled it off.

That is the wrong question.

The change was in her posture. The change was that for the first time in this job, Annie wasn't waiting for instructions, working through a to-do list, or reacting to incoming tasks. *She wasn't handed initiative, she took it.*

Annie crossed a bridge that day. She became someone who starts something, someone who initiates, someone who is prepared to fail along the way if it helps her make a difference.

Your turn

Imagine that the world had no middlemen, no publishers, no bosses, no HR folks, no one telling you what you couldn't do.

If you lived in that world, what would you do?

Go. Do that.

***

In China, there's a factory that can make the same widgets your company makes—for a tenth of the price.

Down the street, there's a restaurant busy stealing your menu and your wine list, but charging 20 percent less than you can charge.

The last travel agent has left the room. Magazine publishers gave up all their growth to bloggers. Wikipedia didn't have to grab the reins of authority from the *Encyclopedia Britannica;* contributors just showed up and did the work. *Britannica* staffers sat and watched.

The intermediaries and agenda setters and investors are less important than they have ever been before. Last year, sixty-seven Web startups in San Francisco and New York were funded for what it costs Silicon Valley to fund a third of that number.

So, if money and access and organizational might aren't the foundation of the connected economy, what is?

Initiative.

This is a manifesto about starting.

Starting a project, making a ruckus, taking what feels like a risk.

Not just "I'm starting to think about it," or "We're going to meet on this," or even "I filed a patent application...."

No, starting.

Going beyond the point of no return.

Leaping.

Committing.

Making something happen.

The seventh imperative

▷ The first imperative is to be aware—aware of the market, of opportunities, of who you are.

▷ The second imperative is to be educated, so you can understand what's around you.

▷ The third imperative is to be connected, so you can be trusted as you engage.

▷ The fourth imperative is to be consistent, so the system knows what to expect.

▷ The fifth imperative is to build an asset, so you have something to sell.

▷ The sixth imperative is to be productive, so you can be well-priced.

But you can do all of these things and still fail. A job is not enough. A factory is not enough. A trade is not enough. It used to be, but no longer.

The world is changing too fast. Without the spark of initiative, you have no choice but to simply react to the world. Without the ability to instigate and experiment, you are stuck, adrift, waiting to be shoved.

I can find a thousand books and a million memos about the first six imperatives. They were drilled into you in countless moments in school, and plenty of graduate schools and bosses are delighted to help you with them. But when it comes to the seventh imperative, it seems as though you're on your own.

The seventh imperative is frightening and thus easy to overlook or ignore. The seventh imperative is to have the guts and the heart and the passion to ship.

The difference of go

The simple thing that separates successful individuals from those who languish is the very thing that separates exciting and growing organizations from those that stagnate and die.

The winners have turned initiative into a passion and a practice. Go ahead, make a list. Make a list of the people and organizations you admire. My guess is the seventh imperative is what sets them apart.

The challenge, it turns out, isn't in perfecting your ability to know when to start and when to stand by. The challenge is getting into the habit of starting.

Craig Ventner and Dr. Frankenstein

The man who sequenced the human genome has figured out how to use a computer to completely design the genetic code of an organism. He and his team can mess with the genes almost as easily as you can edit an essay in Word.

And yet.

And yet once the strand of code is generated and turned into organic matter in a petri dish, it just lies there. It's not alive.

The motive force—the spark that brings it to life—is missing. Ventner still needs to insert some organic tissue, something living, something alive, to transform the project into more than an inert mass of genes.

Surprisingly, that's precisely your opportunity.

Not to buy a petri dish and a bunch of organic materials. No, the opportunity is bigger than that—it's to see that all around you are platforms, opportunities, and entire organizations that will come to life once you are driven enough and brave enough to contribute the initiative they are missing.

The buzzer box

When my cousin was born, my uncle (who has a Ph.D. from MIT) built a buzzer box. It was a heavy metal contraption, with a thick black cord that plugged into the wall. It looked like something from a nuclear power plant, not a kid's toy, but that didn't dissuade him from tossing it into the crib.

The box had two switches, some lights, and a few other controls on it. Flip one switch and a light goes on. Flip both switches and a buzzer sounds. All terrifying, of course, unless you are a kid.

A kid sees the buzzer box and starts poking it. *If I do this, that happens!*

Mathematicians call this a function. Put in one variable, get a result. Call and response.

Life is a buzzer box. Poke it.

The elements of production

Here's what's needed to make something happen:

▷ an idea

▷ people to work on it

▷ a place to build or organize it

▷ raw materials

▷ distribution

▷ money

▷ marketing

These are the inputs that economists have long understood. Go to any business school in the country and you can take courses on any of these elements. Go to Wall Street and you'll find an entire industry devoted to just one of them.

All of this work is wasted if the least understood (but most essential) input is missing. If no one says "go," the project languishes. If no one insists, pushes, creates, cajoles, and launches, then there's nothing; it's all wasted.

My thesis: All of the other elements are cheaper and easier to find than ever before. Which makes the motive force so critical.

We have built the largest economic engine in history. All the tools are here, cheaper than ever before. The market is waiting, the capital is waiting, the factories are waiting, and yes, even the stores are waiting.

They're waiting for someone to say "go."

Walking in circles

Dr. Jan Souman, of the Max Planck Institute for Biological Cybernetics, studied what happens to us when we have no map, no compass, no way to determine landmarks. I'm not talking about a metaphor—he researched what happens to people lost in the woods or stumbling around the Sahara, with no north star, no setting sun to guide them.

It turns out we walk in circles. Try as we might to walk in a straight line, to get out of the forest or the desert, we end up back where we started. Our instincts aren't enough. In the words of Dr. Souman, "Don't trust your senses because even though you might think you are walking in a straight line when you're not."

Human nature is to need a map. If you're brave enough to draw one, people will follow.

Who says yes?

"What do you do here?"

That's a question I often ask people in organizations. It's interesting to hear people describe their roles, their jobs, their sets of tasks. Some people are self-limiting ("I sort the TPS reports every Thursday"), while others are grandiose ("I'm responsible for our culture").

Almost no one says, "I start stuff."

This is astonishing if you think about it. If there's no one starting stuff, then where does innovation come from? Not the ideas; no, there are plenty of those, but the starting. If all that we're missing is the spark of life, the motive force, why is this overlooked?

Where is the VP of starting? How many no's have to be surmounted before you get to a yes? Clearly, there's a guy in charge of the plant or the sales force or the money. But who is in charge of "yes"?

Poke the box

How do computer programmers learn their art? Is there a step-by-step process that guarantees you'll get good?

All great programmers learn the same way. They poke the box. They code something and see what the computer does. They change it and see what the computer does. They repeat the process again and again until they figure out how the box works.

The box might be a computer or it might be a market or it might be a customer or it might be your boss. It's a puzzle, one that can be solved in only one way—by poking.

When you do *this*, what happens? When you do *that*, what happens? The box reveals itself through your poking, and as you get better at it, you not only get smarter but also gain ownership. Ownership doesn't have to be equity or even control. Ownership comes from understanding and from having the power to make things happen.

Doug Rushkoff and Mark Fraunfelder have both written about the new willingness to surrender control to the objects and organizations in our life. As soon as we willingly and blindly accept what's given, we lose all power. Only by poking, testing, modifying, and understanding can we truly own anything, truly exert our influence.

No one has influence, control, or confidence in his work until he understands how to initiate change and predict how the box will respond.

What can you start?

Outsized entrepreneurs are lionized daily. We've heard their names again and again—people (too often men) who started a business, started an organization, started a revolution. Good for them. But you don't have to be Howard Schultz to be an initiator.

People have come to the erroneous conclusion that if they're not willing to start something separate, world-changing, and risky, they have no business starting anything. Somehow, we've fooled ourselves into believing that the project has to have a name, a building, and a stock ticker symbol to matter.

In fact, people within organizations are perfectly situated to start something. The third person in the four-person inbound customer service team can do it. The receptionist can do it. The assistant foreman can do it.

The spark I'm talking about is simple to describe, but easy to avoid.

Is there someone struggling with a tray as she walks across the hospital cafeteria? You can stand up, walk over, and help her. It's not your job, it might not even be appreciated, but you can do it.

Is there a better way to answer the phone when angry customers call? You can try it out and then teach it to others.

Is there a noisy hinge that bothers everyone in the room? You can bring in some oil and fix it.

This is so obvious that it physically hurts me to type it.

If it's so obvious, though, why doesn't everyone do it?

When can you start?

Soon is not as good as now.

Kinds of capital

What can you invest? What can your company invest?

- ▷ Financial capital—Money in the bank that can be put to work on a project or investment.

- ▷ Network capital—People you know, connections you can make, retailers and systems you can plug into.

- ▷ Intellectual capital—Smarts. Software systems. Access to people with insight.

- ▷ Physical capital—Plant and machinery and tools and trucks.

- ▷ Prestige capital—Your reputation.

- ▷ Instigation capital—The desire to move forward. The ability and the guts to say yes.

Think about how prestige and networks and access to capital seduce us. Most screenwriters would prefer to have their film produced by a major movie studio instead of an independent director. There's a bigger pile of resumes from car designers at GM than at Aptera. *The market responds to the power that comes with capital.*

My favorite kind of capital is the last one, of course. It turns out that this is the most important capital of our new economy.

Double double

In a small village, like the one we used to live in, innovation can trump the competition for a long time. The market is sparsely populated, the other organizations are paralyzed with fear, and you can happily leverage an advantage for months or years. For a business to double its pace, double its market share, or double its innovation is sufficient to profit for a generation.

In Google-world, though, the universe of competitors and potential competitors is too high to count—essentially infinite. In a world where news travels instantly and the state of the art is visible to all, the half-life of an insight or an innovation is short and getting shorter.

Doubling is not sufficient. Innovating and then harvesting isn't a long-term strategy. The only defensible way to thrive is to double and then double again. To innovate on the way to innovating, to start on the way to starting yet again.

Not faster, if faster means Lucille Ball on the candy assembly line, stuffing truffles into boxes or her mouth or her blouse as fast as she can, struggling to keep up. No, faster as in shorter cycles, more attention on change, an obsession with changing the status quo merely to see what happens.

Aimless is where we end up when we don't care so much about where we're going, or we try to hide and limit our contributions. I'm pushing for the opposite of that—for "aimful," if you want to coin a phrase.

Is flux the same as risk?

Flux is flow. We can measure the flux of heat or molecular change. Things are moving.

Risk involves winning and losing. We put something at stake, and it might pay off (or it might not).

There is no risk when you put an ice cube in a hot cup of tea. The heat moves from the water to the ice; there's flux... movement.

Risk, to some, is a bad thing, because risk brings with it the possibility of failure. It might be only a temporary failure, but that doesn't matter so much if the very thought of it shuts you down. So, for some, risk comes to equal failure (take enough risks and sooner or later, you will fail). Risk is avoided because we've been trained to avoid failure. I define anxiety as experiencing failure in advance... and if you have anxiety about initiating a project, then of course you will associate risk with failure.

Over time, people have begun to confuse flux with risk as well. We have concluded that if things are flowing, if there is movement, then of course there is risk.

Those who fear risk also begin to fear movement of any kind. People act as though flux, the movement of people or ideas or anything else that's unpredictable, exposes us to risk, and risk exposes us to failure. The fearful try to avoid collisions, so they avoid movement.

These people have made two mistakes. First, they've assumed that risk is a bad thing, and second, they've confused risk and flux, and come to the conclusion that movement is a bad thing as well.

I'm not surprised to discover that many of these people are stuck. Stuck with the status quo, stuck defending their position in the market, stuck with the education they have, unwilling to get more. They are stuck because they are afraid to watch something new on TV, afraid to read something new on their Kindle, afraid to ask a hard question.

None of this would be relevant, except: Now the whole world is in flux. If your project doesn't have movement, then compared to the rest of the world, you're actually moving backward. Like a rock in a flowing river, you might be standing still, but given the movement around you, *collisions are inevitable.*

The irony for the person who prefers no movement is that there's far less turbulence around the log floating down that same river. It's moving, it's changing, but compared to the river around it, it's relatively calm.

The economy demands flux. Flux isn't risky. Flux is what we're in for. Fortunately, flux is also what we were born for.

The trail of failure

"This will end up in crying" was the warning my mom would announce when she encountered a situation between my sisters and me, one that was fraught with sibling misbehavior.

And that's the way some people think about a career built on initiative.

Most things break. Most ideas fail. Most initiatives don't succeed. And if you're the one behind them, if you're the guy who's always starting something that fails, then it seems you're doomed.

After all, our society loves to do the failure dance. (The victory dance, not so much. The victory dance feels like bragging. But the *schadenfreude* of the failure dance—that's just fine.) Watch a football game or listen to the analysis of a political campaign or read a magazine's account of a failed business venture—it's easy for us to point fingers, to find blame, to gleefully critique the things that went wrong.

I need to sell you on why avoiding failure is counterproductive.

First, let's make a list of people who have made a career out of starting (and thus often failing): Harlan Ellison, Steve Carrell, Oprah Winfrey, Richard Wright, Mark Cuban, Mehmet Oz, George Orwell, Michael Bloomberg, Nan Talese, Gloria Steinem, and it goes on and on. In fact, I didn't have to do any research at all to come up with this list; I just wrote down the names of a bunch of famous and respected and successful people.

Oprah has had failed shows, failed projects, failed predictions. She starts something every day, sometimes a few times a day, and there's a long, long list of things that haven't worked out. No one keeps track of that list, though, because the market (and our society) has such respect for the work she's done that *has* succeeded. Mehmet Oz has lost patients. Mark Cuban has backed failed businesses. The more you do, the more you fail.

Second, let's think about the sort of failure we're talking about. Not the failure of disrespect, of the shortcut that shouldn't have been taken or the shoddy work of someone who doesn't care. No, we're talking about the failure of people with good intent, people seeking connection and joy and the ability to make a difference.

No one is suggesting that you wing it in your job at the nuclear power plant, or erratically jump from task to task instead of studying for the upcoming SAT. Hard work is going to be here no matter what. The kind of initiative I'm talking about is difficult because it's important and frightening and new.

If you sign up for the initiative path and continue on it when others fret about "quality" and "predictability," you will ultimately succeed. The crowd won't stop worrying, because worrying is what they enjoy doing. But that's okay, because you'll be making a difference and using your newfound leverage to do more and more work that matters.

The epidemic

So many people are frozen in the face of uncertainty and paralyzed at the thought of shipping work that matters that one might think that it the fear is hardwired into us.

It is.

Scientists can identify precisely where your lizard brain lives. This is your prehistoric early brain, the same brain that's in the lizard or the deer. Filled with fear, intent on reproduction.

Steven Pressfield gives the voice of the lizard brain a name: he calls it the resistance. And the resistance is talking to you as you read this, urging you to compromise, to not be an troublemaker, to avoid rash moves. For many of us, the resistance is always chattering away, frequently sabotaging our best opportunities and ruining our best chance to do great work. Naming it helps you befriend it, and befriending it helps you ignore it.

The first rule of doing work that matters

Go to work on a regular basis.

Art is hard. Selling is hard. Writing is hard. Making a difference is hard.

When you're doing hard work, getting rejected, failing, working it out—this is a dumb time to make a situational decision about whether it's time for a nap or a day off or a coffee break.

Zig Ziglar taught me this twenty years ago. Make your schedule before you start. Don't allow setbacks or blocks or anxiety to push you to say, "hey, maybe I should check my e-mail for a while, or you know, I could use a nap." If you do that, the lizard brain will soon be trained to use that escape hatch again and again.

Isaac Asimov wrote and published more than 400 (!) books by typing nonstop from 6 am to noon, every day for forty years.

The first five years of my solo business, when the struggle seemed never-ending, I never missed a day, never took a nap. (I also committed to ending the day at a certain time and not working on the weekends. It cuts both ways.)

In short: show up.

Naps.google.com

What separates the last five years at Google from those of just about every other successful startup? Compare them to eBay, Yahoo!, Netscape, or About.com.

Simple: After their initial business innovation was proven successful, Google ignored Wall Street. Instead of solely maximizing the yield of their one trick, they continue to invest (some people say over-invest, but those people are wrong) in new tools, new projects, and new ways for people to connect and interact.

Most initiatives fail. That's fine. At least Google's not napping.

Your ego and your project

Somewhere along the way, ego became a nasty word. It's not.

When our name is on a project, our ego pushes us over the hump and drives us to do even better work. Ego drives us to seek acceptance, to make a difference, and to push the envelope. If ego wasn't a key driver in the process, then creative, generous work would all be anonymous, and it isn't.

It's okay. Let your ego push you to be the initiator.

But tell your ego that the best way to get something shipped is to let other people take the credit. The real win for you (and your ego) is seeing something get shipped, not in getting the credit when it does.

Redefining quality

"Good enough" used to be the definition of quality. Your product or service had to be good enough to be considered.

Then the quality revolution hit and the market defined quality as "without defects."

Just about everything on offer—from a car to an iPad to an insurance policy—does exactly what it's supposed to. You turn the key or open the box and it works. Every time.

Things work so often that we're now shocked when a battery dies, a car gets recalled, orr we find a typo in a book.

Most of your competition is now without defects as well—which means that quality is not so interesting anymore. We demand it, but we don't have to seek it out. If you have quality and they have quality and that's all either of you offers, then you're selling a commodity, and I'll take cheap, please.

We have little choice but to move beyond quality and seek remarkable, connected, and new.

Remarkable, as you've already figured out, demands initiative.

Brainwashed by the pit boss

Factories need compliant workers. Casinos need dealers who will do exactly as they are told. NASA needs astronauts who don't question orders on a routine mission. Coal mines need miners who will follow all the instructions, day after day.

Along the way, the factory owners faced a choice. They could trust workers to use their best judgment, to figure things out, to make things better, or they could work to eliminate individual initiative and instead trade the upside of improvement for the certainty of compliance.

You guessed it—many of them chose compliance.

The downside of this choice is now becoming obvious. Factories of all kinds are finding themselves stuck, unable not only to innovate but even to improve. Detroit yelled at auto workers long enough that the union finally said, "fine, we'll just do exactly the minimum." The symphony conductors scolded innovative musicians often enough that they finally said, "fine, we'll play the notes exactly as written." And the mass market rewarded mediocre food companies often enough that they decided to embrace the bland.

The problem: you can't get blander than bland. You can't grow by becoming even more predictable and ordinary. You might have a dependable and predictable and cheap product, but if the market wants something better, you'll be stuck playing catch-up.

Why is this mediocre?

We love to point out how broken our systems are. We enjoy getting angry at hotels or government agencies or airlines that are so obviously doing a poor job. Idiots!

But we almost never look at merely mediocre products and wonder why they aren't great. Mediocre services or products do what they're supposed to, but have set the bar so low that it's hardly worth the energy to cross the street to buy them. A resolute generic sameness pervades this mediocrity.

Why isn't every restaurant meal a fabulous buy for the money? Why isn't every tax dollar spent with the intensity and focus it could be spent with? It seems as though we are willing to accept mediocre as long as the product, the service, or the organization isn't *totally* broken.

There's never a problem getting a posse together to fix the broken. The upside for you (and the challenge) is to find the energy and the will to challenge the mediocre.

When in doubt...

Look for the fear. That's almost always the source of your doubt.

Where did curious go?

If you visit Penguin Magic online, you'll see video after video of stunning mind-reading, metal-bending, shoe-tying magic. And in the videos, the magicians are on the street, performing for passersby. A well-done illusion leads to a lot of screaming. The audience can't believe it. It's a miracle! Satan! And then, curiosity.

"How did you do that?"

Every once in a while, I'll perform an illusion or some technical shortcut and someone won't ask how. People have been indoctrinated so completely by their jobs that they don't want to know how something works, they're willing to accept that perhaps the laws of nature don't work as they expect, and by the way, can I have the remote?

Initiative is a little like creativity in that both require curiosity. Not the search for the "right" answer, as much as an insatiable desire to understand how something works and how it might work better.

The difference is that the creative person is satisfied once he sees how it's done. The initiator won't rest until he does it.

Pick me! Pick me!

The relentless brainwashing of our fading industrial economy has created an expensive misunderstanding. Creative people or those with something to say believe that they have to wait to be chosen.

Authors, for example, wait to be chosen by an agent, and then by a publisher. Then they agitate to be chosen by a media outlet so they can reach readers who will ultimately read their books. Get chosen by Oprah and everything takes care of itself.

Entrepreneurs often find themselves waiting to be chosen by a venture capitalist or investor. They need that selection in order to validate their work and to get started on actually building a business.

Employees wait to be picked for promotion, or to lead a meeting or to speak up at a meeting.

"Pick me, pick me" acknowledges the power of the system and passes responsibility to someone else to initiate. Even better, "pick me, pick me" moves the blame from you to them.

If you don't get picked, it's their fault, not yours.

If you do get picked, well, they said you were good, right? Not your fault anymore.

Reject the tyranny of picked. Pick yourself.

The promoter and the organizer

My friend Jessica wants to be a conference organizer. You can hire her and she'll sweat every single detail of your event. Give her the attendee list, the venue, and the agenda, and the conference will go off without a hitch.

The problem with this plan is that it involves being picked by the event promoter. If she gets picked often, it's a fine living. If she can negotiate a fair payday, it's a fine living. But Jessica must pitch the promoter, hat in hand.

The promoter, on the other hand, has all the power. The promoter initiates the conference. The promoter, who has skills very similar to the organizer's, actually gets to hire the organizer. The promoter is the picker, not the one waiting to get picked.

So... why not be the promoter, the initiator, the one in charge and responsible?

Over the years, Jerry Weintraub earned more than a hundred million dollars as a promoter, resisting the temptation to sit back and merely react to offers instead. He initiated projects; he didn't sell to them.

Entrepreneurship is merely a special case

It's easy to come to the conclusion that someone who initiates and is willing to challenge the status quo is automatically an entrepreneur, that this is a practice reserved for the boss. We reassure ourselves that since we've given up the reins to the boss or the founder, it's her job to poke, not ours.

In fact, while entrepreneurs initiate, they also do something altogether different: they use money (often belonging to someone else) to build a profitable business that's bigger than themselves. The goal of the entrepreneur is to build an entity, something that can grow and thrive once it's moving. And that's a fabulous prospect, one that requires plenty of guts and initiative.

Entrepreneurship is a special case not because it requires initiative (all of us are required to bring that to the table now) but because it involves using money, people, and assets to create a new, bigger, entity.

Don't make the mistake of believing, though, that everyone else is left with a cog job. Smart entrepreneurs understand that a thriving organization needs more than one person creating change. Nonprofits and even government agencies have discovered that the best way to thrive in a world that's changing is to change, and that happens only when someone is willing to poke the box and see what works.

The season's pass

Ski resorts are happy to sell you a ticket to ski all year, for about the cost of seven days' worth of lift tickets. The people who take the leap and buy the ticket have realized that it's easier (and cheaper) to decide once than it is to make a choice again and again all season.

Initiation is like that. Instead of initiating on an ad hoc basis, worrying each time, getting permission each time, selling each time, why not buy a season's pass? Why not sell your boss or your colleagues on being the initiator? It's your job. You start things. Ask once, do many.

No free lunch

Of course, the challenge of being the initiator is that you'll be wrong. You'll pick the wrong thing, you'll waste time, you'll be blamed.

This is why being an initiator is valuable.

Most people shy away from the challenge. They've been too abused, they're too fearful, they hold back, they're happy to let someone else take the heat.

Initiative is scarce.

Hence valuable.

Ditch digging is not scarce. It's not hard at all to find manual labor at minimum wage, which is precisely why manual labor gets paid minimum wage.

It's extremely difficult to find smart people willing to start useful projects. Because sometimes what you start doesn't work. The fact that it doesn't work every time should give you confidence, because it means you're doing something that frightens others.

Check-in, Chicken

One way to start every morning with your team is to have everyone check in. Go around in a circle and let people update and contribute. It's not a silly exercise if it helps people speak up and it communicates forward motion.

Another way, probably a better one, is to have each member of the team announce what he's afraid of. Two kinds of afraid, actually. Things that might fail and things that might work.

What are you, chicken?

Yes, we're chicken. We're afraid. The lizard has us by the claws.

So, tell us. What are you afraid might happen that would destroy, disintegrate, or dissuade—that would take us down? And what are you afraid of that might work, thus changing everything and opening up entirely new areas of scariness?

The lizard misunderstands the economics of poking

The formula is simple:

When the cost of poking the box (ptb) is less than the cost of doing nothing (ø), then you should poke! $[ptb < ø \longrightarrow poke]$

If you run a giant, billion-dollar steel mill, I don't think you should shut it down for a month to try a new, untested technology.

When you're writing a screenplay, on the other hand, the cost of an innovation is far less than the cost of being boring. Because boring, though it occasionally, randomly, miraculously leads to a sale, almost always fails instead. The cost of being wrong is less than the cost of doing nothing.

Same thing goes for just about any sales, marketing, human resources, software, or management innovation. Same thing goes for just about any interaction you can have with a vendor, client, or co-worker. And that's what most of us do, most of the time. Not run a steel mill.

The connected economy of ideas demands that we contribute initiative. And yet we resist, because our lizard brain, the one that lives in fear, relentlessly exaggerates the cost of being wrong.

Polish this!

Every few minutes, his cell phone chimes.

Apparently, my friend has set the phone to chime every time one of the people he follows on Twitter posts something. This gives him the chance to read it and respond, making him, presumably, a truly valuable follower. He's hoping that polishing his relationships in this way will act as a form of networking, making him more integrated into the Tweeters' lives and perhaps businesses.

All this polishing.

Stand on an urban street corner and you can see it happening. Dozens of ostensibly busy people, staring at their palms and their fingers, polishing their relationships.

The challenge is that it's asymptotic. Twice as much polishing isn't twice as good. Ten times as much polishing is definitely not ten times as good. Whether you're polishing a piece of furniture or an idea, the benefits diminish quickly. The polishing turns into stalling.

I wonder what would happen if instead of rushing to Twitter, my friend used that chime to do something original or provocative or important? What if the chime was his reminder not to polish, but to create?

The Semmelweis Imperative

Poking successfully also requires tact. You're trying to change things, not have people recoil in anger or fear from your poking.

Ignaz Semmelweis was a physician practicing in Hungary during the 1800s. His insight was that poor hygiene by doctors, particularly a lack of hand washing, was the cause of significant disease and death. Despite devoting his life to spreading this news, he died a failure, unpopular and ineffective.

In a book published in 1861, Semmelweis recapped, "Most medical lecture halls continue to resound with lectures on epidemic childbed fever and with discourses against my theories ... in 1854 in Vienna, the birthplace of my theory, 400 maternity patients died from childbed fever."

Why? If the results of his simple intervention were so profound, why did doctors and the medical establishment so completely reject it?

Two reasons. First, he never worked to explain the science. Without a why, without an explanation, it was hard to give his ideas the momentum needed to get them to spread.

Second, as reported by Atul Gawande in *Better*, Semmelweis was a jerk. Impressed by his insight, he never bothered to persuade, or even to be patient. To one doctor, he wrote, "You, Herr Professor, have been a partner in this massacre." To another, "...I declare before God and the world that you are a murderer."

Poke, but be smart about it. After his first insight, for whatever reason, Semmelweis stopped shipping, stopped working to make a difference in the world. Instead of pushing to do what worked, he walked away and never made the impact he could have contributed.

Welcome to Project World

You've been living in Project World for so long you've probably forgotten that for a long time, projects didn't matter so much.

Ford Motor changed the world with a venture that lasted longer than almost any employee in the company did. The Model T came off the assembly line for nineteen years. Ford ultimately sold more than 15 million cars. The people who were there when it launched were probably not the same people who made the cars when the project ceased. Sure, it was a project to get the car launched, but the real job of Ford Motor was to make a lot of this particular model, over and over and over, and profit each time. The project of launching it was a necessary evil, but the large-scale manufacturing was their business.

Consider the organizations you've encountered, bought from, or worked for. Most of them (if they've been around for more than a decade or two) are based on this assembly line model of scalability. *The system is the system; don't mess with it.*

Now, think about the newer organizations, the ones that are growing and making an impact. Think about Apple, Google, director James Cameron's team, Ideo, Pixar, and Electronic Arts. These are project-centric organizations. Each one of these organizations consists of groups of committed people who ship projects.

No projects, no organization. Coasting isn't an option because projects don't last forever. The people stick around, the posture persists, but the projects need to be refreshed. After a project is shipped, there's no useful work until someone starts a new project.

As organizations have begun to coalesce around projects, they've made a startling discovery: the starting part is harder than it looks.

How to invent and choose and stick with or abandon ideas, how to select and predict and forecast the future of a project—this is all difficult.

And it begins with the initiator, the one who begins things.

The Ford System is dead, long live the Ford System

Henry Ford figured out that productivity was the secret to market success. Make cars more efficiently and you can sell them far cheaper. Cheaper cars will outsell expensive ones of similar quality.

And so he perfected the factory system based on obedience, interchangeable parts, and interchangeable people.

That system has no growth left in it. It has moved overseas (not just for cars, but for so many things we buy), and even in low-cost factories around the world, organizations are finding out that you can't cut prices forever.

The new system, then, the one embraced by the new Ford and by so many other organizations, is to use the stable, productive business platform we've developed to produce *things*, and continue to build *projects* on that platform. The new system doesn't consume oil or electricity on an assembly line; it thrives on innovation. Call it a project line.

The old system can't work without the new. And the new system depends on unpredictable human beings adding unscheduled insights.

What happened to Excellence?

Tom Peters changed everything when he decided to devote his life to spreading the word about the ideas in *In Search of Excellence*. Over twenty-five years, he's traveled millions of miles and given thousands of talks.

I can see the frustration in his eyes when he's on stage. While millions of people have embraced the thinking behind his work, too many others are still waiting for him to tell them exactly what to do. They don't understand that Excellence isn't about working extra hard to do what you're told. It's about taking the initiative to do work you decide is worth doing.

This is a revolutionary overthrow of time and motion studies, of foremen, of bureaucracies and bosses. It's not a new flavor of the old soup. It's a personal, urgent, this-is-my-call/this-is-my-calling way to do your job.

Please stop waiting for a map. We reward those who draw maps, not those who follow them.

Business development

Many organizations have a bizdev team. Not quite marketing, not quite sales, these are the folks responsible for the new deals, partnerships, and transformative ideas. It's the bizdev team that finds a new toy for McDonald's kids' meals, or a new way to use shelf space at Starbucks.

The bizdev team has no fixed agenda, no easy way to decide what's next. The bizdev team is in charge of starting things.

Most organizations need this capability, but few have it. Those that do are often world-class bad at it, because no one on the team has the posture of initiation. Everyone is afraid to poke too hard, afraid to reach out, stand up, and create the new.

What next?

How often do our heroes stand still? It's hard to imagine Spock and Kirk landing on a planet and just relaxing for a month or two.

Just hanging out has nothing to do with boldly going where no one has gone before.

What differentiates us from every other creature is that we go places, places we've not gone before. We do it willingly, and often. What makes our work and our life interesting is discovery, surprise, and the risk of exploration. (Insert Monty Python Spanish Inquisition insider riff here.)

The factory has programmed that adventurous impulse out of us. The economic imperative of the last century has been to avoid risk, avoid change, and most of all, avoid exploration and the new. An efficient factory fears change because change means retooling and risk and a blip in productivity. Sure, we'll put up with change if we have to, and welcome the predictable incremental change of productivity improvement, but please leave us alone when it comes to the word "bold."

Avoiding risk worked then but doesn't work now.

Now "what's next?" is in fact the driving force for individuals and for organizations. Ever onward, ever faster.

If you see something, say something

Do we actually need this slogan and the ads that go with it?

Let's deconstruct it for a second:

If you see something (something: a dangerous device, a bomb, say, or a zombie with a knife, or a suitcase with sparks coming out of it, or asbestos hanging from the ceiling of the day care center), say something (something: pick up the phone, dial 9-1-1, point it out to a soldier in camouflage).

Why would anyone hesitate to report a zombie?

Because we've been taught to shut up and keep our heads down. Because the authorities don't actually like gadflies or neighborhood-watch busybodies. So they make it uncomfortable to speak up. In many police departments, the first suspect in a dispute is the one who took the time to call it in.

This slogan is one more example of the amplification of society's instinct to ignore instead of act.

Allowed (not allowed)

Most employees can give you a long list of all the things they're not allowed to do. Not-allowed lists exist in schools, in relationships, and in jobs. The park near my house doesn't allow dogs, non-residents, or birthday parties.

It's interesting that the allowed list is harder to remember and to write down. I think we might be afraid of how much freedom we actually have, and how much we're expected to do with that freedom.

It's comforting to live with a list of what's not allowed. We remember it, we push against it, but ultimately, we enjoy the confinement that the limits bring us. When revolutions appear, when the list gets much shorter, it's surprising how long it takes for us to take action. Simple example: how long did it take after the birth of blogs or Twitter for you to begin speaking up? Before this, you had no cheap, easy, allowable way to speak your mind to the world. You weren't allowed.

Then you were.

And yet most people who use these tools took years (!) to take action and start.

The death of idealism

Sooner or later, many idealists transform themselves into disheartened realists who mistakenly believe that giving up is the same thing as being realistic.

When they start out, the idealists believe that doing something is far better than doing nothing. They understand the system, the process, the way it's all set up to work. They want to fix it, change it, or at least disturb it.

Over time, these politicians, entrepreneurs, or activists discover that as they get more leverage, they seem to give up the very thing that got them into this position in the first place. The people arguing on behalf of accepting the status quo are the ones who, years ago, set out to change it.

For so many people, this transformation is preventable.

As disillusionment sets in, people stop poking. They find themselves slowing down, dissuaded or disheartened, so they start to accept the status quo. The irony is that the act of creating and shipping remarkable ideas is the very thing that can change the status quo. Yelling at the cable TV anchor never changed anything. Yell long enough and you'll merely end up hoarse.

The alternative is to relentlessly and consistently be starting something (and finishing it). Julie Taymor, Alice Waters, and Sarah Jones could all sit back and become one of those disillusioned realists. Instead, like everyone who is making a difference, they continue to poke. It's a choice.

Don't tell Woodie

My dog wears one of those Invisible Fence collars. There's a wire around our small yard, and if she gets near it, her collar buzzes. If she goes a bit farther, she gets a small shock. (I think she's been shocked exactly once.) The dog associates the buzz with the shock and never goes near the edge.

The thing is, the wire broke a year ago, so the system doesn't work. But Woodie now associates the collar with the behavior, and leaves the yard only if we take the collar off.

The boundary is in her head, not in the system.

I wonder what would happen...

None of this works without curiosity.

Success-minded people have no trouble at all following proven instructions. We all would be happy to follow a map if the map came with a guarantee.

There is no guarantee, though. There are no maps. They've all been taken, and their value is not what it used to be, because your competitors have maps, too.

The opportunity lies in pursuing your curiosity instead. Curiosity is not allergic to failure. Curiosity drives us to the haunted house because the thrills lie in what we don't expect, not in what's safe.

Curiosity can start us down the path to shipping, to bringing things to the world, to examining them, refining them, and repeating the process again (and again).

Three thousand TED talks

The original TED conference featured scientific and literary giants (and some politicians, too). It wasn't much of a surprise when the series of talks they did became an Internet sensation.

The fascinating part came later, when Chris Anderson and the TED team invited people all over the world to run their own versions of TED. Called TEDx, these are independently run conferences featuring speakers from every line of work, most of whom have traditional jobs.

Three thousand talks later, it's pretty clear that big ideas and unsettling concepts are not just the work of people who get paid to think that way.

In fact, we're all capable of poking the box. In every country and in most industries, there are passionate people who are making a difference. Because they can.

If you had a chance to do a TED talk, what would it be about? What have you discovered, what do you know, what can you teach? You should do one. Even if you don't do one, you should be prepared to do one.

That's your opportunity—to approach your work in a way that generates unique learning and interactions that are worth sharing.

The Joy of Wrong

In the Pike Place Market in Seattle, you can still find the first Starbucks. There's something wrong with it, though. It's not quite right, not quite a Starbucks. The logo is different; the layout is different.

It turns out that the original Starbucks didn't sell coffee.

They sold coffee beans and tea leaves and even herbs. But except for a sip or a taste of coffee brewed from a particular bean (drip, no espresso!), there was no cup of coffee to be had.

Starbucks was wrong. Jerry Baldwin, one of the founders, made a mistake. He thought the beans were the point, not the coffee. Left to Jerry's vision of the future, Starbucks would certainly have failed. It took Howard Schultz, a trip to Italy, and an obsession with espresso to turn Starbucks into Starbucks. And Howard gets a lot of credit for making that happen.

But what if the "wrong" Starbucks had never been built? What if Jerry and his partners had said, "Well, we're not sure if this bean thing is going to work, so let's do nothing"? Without Jerry Baldwin and his flawed idea for a coffee bean store, there'd be no Frappuccino. One led to the other by the usual route, which is never a straight line.

The original Starship Enterprise was conceived by Matt Jefferies. It looked like a cross between a Frisbee and a can opener. Clearly wrong.

But Matt had the drive to deliver. He took the wrong start and revised and improved and innovated until the Enterprise we know and love came to be. The hardest part, it seems to me, was the first one, the wrong one.

Poking doesn't mean right. It means action.

The world is a lot more complicated than it appears

Google finds you the right answer, apparently, after a two-word search of 12 billion pages.

A blogger outlines exactly what to do in three paragraphs.

A book gives you the thirteen steps to achieve your dreams.

The company policy manual has an answer for your situation, and it only takes a few vice presidents to make it clear.

It's enough to persuade you that all the answers are here, and that all we need from you is compliance.

There are two forces arguing for accepting the presented answers. The first force is the industrial age, which pushes us to make immediate choices at work because there's just no time for indecision when there are machines just waiting and markets just waiting and people on the line just waiting.

The second force is the digital age, because computers like matches and decision trees and on or off. They don't like maybe.

Initiative and starting are about neither of these. They are about "let's see" and "try."

If there's no clear right answer, perhaps the thing you ought to do is something new. Something new is often the right path when the world is complicated.

Rote

"I don't know what's the matter with people: they don't learn by understanding, they learn by some other way—by rote or something. Their knowledge is so fragile!"

—Richard Feynman

"This might not work"

Is it okay to say these four words?

Is your work so serious and flawless and urgent that each thing you do, every day, must work?

Change is powerful, but change always comes with failure as its partner. "This might not work" isn't merely something to be tolerated; it's something you should seek out.

Attempt

One of my earliest memories is of going to the Ringling Bros. Circus with my grandmother. We sat in the darkened Madison Square Garden, swinging those little lights on a string around and around. The ringmaster intoned (he didn't announce, he intoned), "Ladies and gentlemen, in the center ring, high above you on the trapeze, they will now attempt a triple flip...."

The way he said *attempt* led us all to believe that this might not work. Attempt. Not perform. Not display. We weren't there to see the acrobats do something great that they had done again and again. No, we were going to see something new, something risky, something interesting.

Only in systems where quality is a given do we care about attempts. I'm not sure Yoda was right when he said, "Do or do not, there is no try." Yes, there is a try. Try is the opposite of hiding.

Take a lid off it

Implicit in all of my ranting about poking is this: You already have good ideas, already have something to say, already have a vivid internal dialogue about what you could do and how it might make things better.

If you don't, if there's just static inside, I think it's really unlikely you read this far.

For the rest of us, the majority of us, there's an engine running on "better." We have a daemon in our head, a voice that often starts with "what about..." and then trails off, disgusted at our inability to actually try this stuff out, to poke.

The reasons for lying low are clear and obvious and stupid. The opportunity is to adopt a new practice, one where you find low-risk, low-cost ways to find out just how smart and intuitive and generous you actually are.

Starting implies (demands) finishing

What's the distinction between carrying around a great idea, being a brainstormer, tinkering—and starting something?

Starting means you're going to finish. If it doesn't ship, you've failed. You haven't poked the box if the box doesn't realize it's been poked.

To merely start without finishing is just boasting, or stalling, or a waste of time. I have no patience at all for people who believe they are doing their best work but are hiding it from the market. If you don't ship, you actually haven't started anything at all. At some point, your work has to intersect with the market. At some point, you need feedback as to whether or not it worked. Otherwise, it's merely a hobby.

Notions belong in the sewing store, not in your work

We all have notions, inklings, and even strong hunches. Playing with hunches is not the same as poking the box.

If you keep the idea inside you, you are merely hypothetically shipping, conceptually testing the market, prototyping your concept.

If you don't finish, it doesn't really count as starting, and if you don't start, you're not poking.

Shipping and fear

In an environment that values shipping, one that makes things happen, it becomes perversely more difficult for some people to start something. That's because the odds that something you start will actually get finished and hit the market will increase dramatically.

It's one thing to amuse oneself by pitching clever ideas to someone who will never take action, and another to say things to someone who has a history of actually doing something about it. The writers at *Saturday Night Live* quickly discover that something they say on Wednesday might be seen by 10 million people just a few days later. Some people respond to this by saying less, by self-censoring, by holding back. And some view it as the chance of a lifetime.

Writing this manifesto might be overwhelming. I know it's going to be read, at least by a few people. If I focus on that—focus on the fact that yes, it will be seen and criticized and worked with and misunderstood and embraced and spread—then I'm bound to hold back. The challenge is to focus on the work, not on the fear that comes from doing the work.

As you get better at shipping, you may notice that your ability to instigate starts to fade. The knowledge that your idea might turn into something is paralyzing. It means that your notions and hunches must face more self-scrutiny. So the new manager says to herself, "I better not tell my staff that pickles are the trendy new appetizer, or they'll be on the menu within days—and if they flop, the buck will stop with me."

The initiator as outsider

Society isn't kind to those who don't fit in. We ostracize, we call names, we harass.

Part of the indoctrination that leads to conformity comes from this social pressure. *Dilbert* is a daily reminder of how hard organizations work to maintain the status quo.

Smart organizations have figured out how to turn the standard—the expectation of stasis—on its head. At fast-moving organizations, the best way to become an insider, a leader, someone who matters, is to initiate.

At every job of mine that I've liked, I've found a culture where the spark of initiation was valued. Unfortunately, too many places are stuck with a culture of stasis.

Jim thinks I have a crazy brain

Jim Walberg sent me a nice note, thanking me for the contributions of my crazy brain. He's been using the Shipit workbook to get his team members off their chairs and into the business of shipping their ideas.

Of course, my brain is not any crazier than yours. At least I hope not.

The only difference is that I've had a lot of practice in poking the box, figuring out which ideas resonate, and then shipping them. The more you do it, the more it gets done and the less crazy you feel.

Winning the Halloween contest (now vs. later)

In my town every year, there's a treasured family event. Parents and their young kids are given some tempura paint and challenged to paint a storefront's plate glass window. The best 2-foot by 3-foot window mural wins a prize.

The easy way to win is to tell your kid what to do and merely fool the judges (and your kid) into thinking that the painting is the work of a youngster.

The easy way to have your kid lose is to sit there, not speaking, not painting, waiting for your child to pick up the brush and paint something.

The easy way may be the best plan in the short run, but it certainly doesn't work for the long haul.

In the short run, playing your strongest player, following the playbook, rewarding someone who has done it before—these are all great ways to win. In the long run, though, all you've done is taught conformity and punished initiation.

One reason organizations get stuck is that they stick with their "A" players so long that they lose their bench. In a world that's changing, a team with no bench strength and a rigid outlook on the game will always end up losing.

The kid who made a ruckus

Kids initiate. They create situations. They start ruckuses. All of them.

Left to his own devices, the ruckus-causing initiator will continue to do so, forever. He won't stop at five or ten or twenty years old. The essence of being human is to initiate.

But we're not left to our own devices. We are smothered by parents, snubbed by peers, scolded by teachers, organized by authorities, hired by factories, and brainwashed, relentlessly brainwashed to cease any troublesome behavior.

So we do (most of us).

Except for those who don't. The ones who don't—the troublemakers, starters, instigators, questioners, and innovators—are still busy starting things, big and small.

And just in time.

As the economy shifts, large (and small) organizations are discovering that this brainwashing thing was a huge error. You can't snooze your way to greatness. You can't optimize your way to surprising growth. You can't organize your way into blamelessness.

We can unbrainwash ourselves while there's still time.

"The best thing I ever done"

Forty-six years ago, Domenico DeMarco was walking down Avenue J in Brooklyn. He says that he saw all the foot traffic, all the people, and a store for rent on the corner. He grabbed it, on the spot, and opened a pizza place.

Every day since then, he's made every single pizza himself, with his own hands. Every day, Dom DeMarco ships his art, hand to hand, directly to people who appreciate his work. He views each pizza as a new project, not as a widget on an assembly line. He might be seen by some as merely a journeyman, someone who makes pizza (slowly) for not a lot of money. I see him very differently. Dom starts with the simplest elements of his craft and converts them into a personal connection, hundreds of times a day.

What would Dom's life have been like if he had spent more time thinking about and evaluating and studying whether or not this handcrafted life's work was a good idea?

How did you end up with this job?

Almost any time I ask someone that question, they answer with, "well, it's a funny story." And it's not usually a funny story.

Instead, it's a story that juxtaposes a few unlikely breaks with unadorned initiative. People get good gigs because they stand up.

Annie Duke is a former World Series of Poker champion. She has won more than $4 million playing poker professionally.

The interesting question to ask someone in this line of work is: how?

How did you get into it? How did you get good at it?

Hint: you don't get picked.

Annie was broke, living in Montana and trying to figure out how to make ends meet. Encouraged by her brother, she went to a poker game in Billings. No permit, no permission slip, no connection to the game. She won two thousand dollars.

At this point in most poker careers, the winner takes the money, goes home, and goes back to work. There isn't a career because there isn't persistence. There isn't a career because as soon as there's a big loss, it ends. That didn't happen to Annie Duke. Annie set out to fail often enough to get good. She approached the challenge as a professional would. She studied, budgeted, and failed. Often.

Is there a better way? Probably not.

The person who fails the most usually wins

Probably worth unpacking this a little bit.

If you fail *once*, and big, you don't fail the most. The game is over, you're a failure, you're busted, you're in jail. But you don't fail the most.

If you *never* fail, either you're really lucky or you haven't shipped anything.

But if you succeed often enough to be given the privilege of failing next time, then you're on the road to a series of failures. Fail, succeed, fail, fail, fail, succeed—you get the idea.

Talk to any successful person. He'll be happy to fill you in on his long string of failures.

I started a record label, and failed. I started a fundraising business based on light bulbs, and failed. Launched the first aquarium on a VHS tape and failed. Published many books and failed.

The winning part? I learned from each of these failures.

Juggling is about throwing, not catching

That's why it's so difficult to learn how to juggle. We're conditioned to make the catch, to hurdle whatever is in our way to save the day, to—no matter what—not drop the ball.

If you spend your time and energy and focus on catching, it's inevitable that your throws will suffer. You'll get plenty of positive feedback for the catches you make, but you'll always be behind, because the throws you manage to make will be ever less useful.

Paradoxically, if you get better at throwing, the catches take care of themselves.

The only way to get better at throwing, though, is to throw. Throw poorly, throw again. Throw well, throw again. Get good at throwing first.

A paradox of success

People with no credibility or resources rarely get the leverage they need to bring their ideas to the world.

People with credibility and resources are so busy trying to hold onto them that they fail to bring their provocative ideas to the world.

The greatest challenge any successful organization faces is finding the guts to risk that success in order to accomplish something great. And risking that success ultimately becomes the only way to accomplish something great.

What a relief to Bob Dylan when he was booed at the Newport Folk Festival. There, that's out of the way. Now let's make some art.

What a relief to Elizabeth Gilbert when *Committed* didn't sell as well as *Eat, Pray, Love*. There, that's out of the way; now I can write again.

Identifying the sophomore slump, the second-album problem, the challenge of expectations—and then confronting the boss or the shareholders with it, writing it down, talking it up, and relentlessly working to destroy it—is the best way to get back to the reason you set out to do whatever it is you do in the first place.

How to walk to Cleveland

Shipping is an event. There's life before you ship and then there's the moment you ship. And then there's life after you ship.

Starting isn't like that. Starting something is not an event; it's a series of events.

You decide to walk to Cleveland. So you take a first step in the right direction. That's starting. You spend the rest of the day walking toward Cleveland, one step at a time, picking your feet up and putting them down. At the end of the day, twenty miles later, you stop at a hotel.

And what happens the next morning?

Either you quit the project or you start again, walking to Cleveland. In fact, every step is a new beginning. Sure, you're closer than you were yesterday or last week, but you're still heading toward Cleveland.

Keep starting until you finish.

The go of science

During a two-year period, a small team in Palo Alto, CA, invented the laser printer, the high-resolution screen, the mouse, on-screen windows, and even the frame buffer that led to all special effects in the movies. All of it, in twenty-four months.

Was there something in the water?

Sort of.

What this team had was the expectation of initiation. You couldn't be a star at PARC unless you started something audacious.

That's the way all great science works. An individual does something audacious, something counter to the status quo, pursuing a journey that seems ridiculous at first.

The Fear of Wrong

It's not surprising that we hesitate. Starting maximizes the chances of ending up wrong.

Here's the nightmare, and it's a vivid one: The boss finds someone who did something wrong and she hassles/disciplines/humiliates/fires her.

If you're not wrong, that's not going to happen.

On the other hand, there's the other scenario: The boss finds someone who didn't start, who never starts, who always studies or criticizes or plays devil's advocate, and she hassles/disciplines/humiliates/fires her.

Oh, forgive me for teasing you; that never happens.

The typical factory-centric organization places a premium on not-wrong, and spends no time at all weeding out those who don't start.

In the networked economy, the innovation-focused organization has no choice but to obsess about those who don't start.

Today, not starting is far, far worse than being wrong. If you start, you've got a shot at evolving and adjusting to turn your wrong into a right. But if you don't start, you never get a chance.

10,000 hours, hard work, and an overnight success

Hollerado is a band you might have just discovered. But they've been poking the box for ages. Here's a letter they sent to blogger Bob Lefsetz (I edited it just a bit):

> We come from a small town in Ontario called Manotick. We have been touring relentlessly for 4 years.
>
> For our first American tour, no-one wanted to book us. So, instead of booking shows, we drove as far away from our homes in Canada as we could get. We would then show up at venues where a show was going on and tell them we were 2,000 miles away from home, had a gig booked down the street but it somehow fell through. "Would you guys mind if we played a short set here tonight?" IT WORKED! We played countless shows this way.
>
> Since we rarely got paid more than a few drinks and sometimes pizza, we needed to make gas money. We had a laptop with the tracks to our demo CD. We would go to Best Buy, get a CD burner and a couple spindles of blank CDs. We

would burn a hundred demos in the parking lot and then return the CD burner to Best Buy. We would then put the demos in Ziploc bags. (Hence the name of our first record... record in a bag.)

Once we had a stash of demos, we would drive to the nearest mall and set up shop in front of Hot Topic (probably the most shameless thing we have done for our band). We would stand there for hours, with discmen and demos, asking anyone who would stop to take a listen if they wanted to buy a demo in a bag. We could sell the discs for 5 bucks and still make $4.50 to put towards gas.

We did this for 2 years. Anything to avoid having a real job, right? In February of 2009, we released our first full-length album for FREE online.

That same month we invented the RESIDENCY TOUR. We took the old concept of playing a residency one day a week at the same bar and made it psycho. We booked 7 residencies for the month, one for each night of the week. Every Sunday of that cold February, we played in at the same club in Boston, every Monday at Piano's in NYC, Tuesday was Lacolle Quebec, Wednesdays - Hamilton Ontario, Thursdays - Toronto, Friday - Ottawa, Saturday - Montreal. Repeat 4 times. 28 shows in a row. Over 12,000 miles of crap Canadian winter driving in 28 days.

In February 2010, we started our own record label to release "record in a bag" in stores in Canada. Although every distributor we talked to said it was impossible, we were finally able to convince one (Arts and Crafts) that we could literally package "record in a bag" in a Ziploc bag filled with goodies. So far we have sold over 10,000 copies of it in Canada. With no label support, our first single, "Juliette," went top 5 in mainstream Canadian alternative radio.

Things began to take hold in Canada and we soon became privy to the Canadian grant system for touring acts. Still, when they gave us a budget to play a showcase in China, we took the budget and stretched it for all it was worth. We turned it into a 3-week tour deep into China. We recorded a song in Mandarin Chinese and released it on the Internet in China. We were able to return for another tour 6 months later.

We can play our instruments. We play live and we play live a lot, hundreds of shows a year, we sweat. We take requests. We play covers we don't know. We play for the audience, as much as for each other, because without them we would still be back in Manotick, working jobs we hated. We play anywhere anytime. It is what we love more than anything.

We are four best friends (2 of the guys are brothers). We intend to do this for a long time. We want to have careers and catalogues that we can be proud of. Personally, I think our song for the video you talked about is not nearly our strongest. Since then we have written a whole bunch more, and like anything else, they are getting better with practice.

My punchline: Four years of doing something new, seeing what works, and doing it again. And again. The music business is hard, and these guys are working it. At the same time, typical bands are still playing some coffeehouse down the street and whining about how hard it is to get a label to discover them.

The market is obsessed with novelty

So go make some. We're tired of your old stuff.

Organizing for joy

Traditional corporations, particularly large-scale service and manufacturing businesses, are organized for efficiency. Or consistency. But not joy.

Joy comes from surprise and connection and humanity and transparency and new. These are alien concepts in many places.

McDonald's, Hertz, Dell, and others crank it out. They show up. They lower costs. They use a stopwatch to measure output.

The problem with this mindset is that as you approach the asymptote of maximum efficiency, there's not a lot of room left for improvement. Making a Chicken McNugget for .00001 cents less isn't going to boost your profit a whole lot.

Worse, the nature of the work is inherently unremarkable. If you fear special requests, if you staff with cogs, if you have to put it all in a manual, then the chances of amazing someone are really quite low.

These organizations have people who will try to patch problems over after the fact, instead of motivated people eager to delight on the spot.

The alternative, it seems, is to organize for joy. These are the companies that give their people the freedom (and the expectation) that they will create, connect, and surprise. These are the organizations that embrace someone who makes a difference, as opposed to searching the employee handbook for a rule that was violated.

Not sure I'm being as clear as I could be: The relentless act of invention and innovation and initiative is the best marketing asset.

To be really clear

I'm not encouraging you to be bold and right. I'm not encouraging you to figure out how to always initiate a smart and proven and profitable idea.

I'm merely encouraging you to start. Often. Forever. Be the one who starts things.

How to do vs. what to do

We often turn to authors and experts for instruction on what to do. If we only knew what to do, the thinking goes, then we'd do it.

I'm not seeing a shortage of what-to-do knowledge. There are plenty of really smart, well-trained people in organizations large and small who know exactly what to do.

The shortage is in people willing to do it. To take a leap. To walk out onto the ledge and start. Apparently, many of us have forgotten *how* to do it.

There is no "just" in "just do it"

The problem with the Nike slogan is the implication that all you have to do to take initiative is to take initiative—that it's merely a matter of will. For some of us, it might be, but for others, it takes more than that.

You're not a starter because you haven't been sold on the idea, haven't been trained in doing it, and haven't been rewarded consistently enough to get into the habit.

Now that you know what's at stake, the next steps are up to you.

The Adventures of Andre and Wally B

In 1984, a filmmaker named John Lasseter started working with a new computer animation tool. The movie he made, *The Adventures of Andre and Wally B*, was a digital short, originally designed to entertain his son.

The movie freaked his young son out. It wasn't turned into a feature film. It didn't make any money, either.

Was starting a mistake? How badly did he fail?

John has been nominated for six Academy awards, has won two, and was a key man in the evolution of Pixar, the most successful film production company of all time. No one else is even close.

John starts things.

The space between the frames

In *Understanding Comics*, Scott McCloud explains not just how comic books work, but how life works.

The secret of the comics isn't what you see in each frame. It's the little gutter, the space in between the frames. Because the artist doesn't draw it in, that space is left up to you. It pulls you in. You create the narrative as the story moves along.

Go read some comics and you'll see. Go ahead, I'll wait.

One thing that most comic artists avoid is showing decisions. They show action, sure, and they show results, but they don't show (because it's difficult to show) the hero or the villain making a choice.

And it's this between-the-frame action that makes poking the box so powerful. Action is easy once you have a plan. Formulating a plan, however, is a rare and valuable skill.

Why growth happens early

Robert Litan of the Brookings Institution points out that almost all real job growth occurs in the first five years after a company's founding. That makes sense, actually. Once a company hits stability, they usually start replacing workers, not inventing new jobs.

During the early days, though, no one is sure of exactly what needs to be done. It's not a job; it's a passion, a mission, and an experiment. The staff is mixed up, confused, and cross-pollinating like mad, trying to survive. When an initiative starts to work, the company hires in that direction. They keep floundering and initiating until they get big enough to relax. And then they stop.

Companies that grow after year five do so because they embrace the discipline of poking.

The right thing to do

I hope we can agree that there's a moral obligation to be honest, to treat people with dignity and respect, and to help those in need.

I wonder if there's also a moral obligation to start.

I believe there is. I believe that if you've got the platform and the ability to make a difference, then this goes beyond "should" and reaches the level of "must." You must make a difference or you squander the opportunity. Wasting the opportunity both degrades your own ability to contribute and, more urgently, takes something away from the rest of us.

Once you've engaged with an organization or a relationship or a community, you owe it to your team to start. To initiate. To be the one who makes something happen.

To do less is to steal from them.

If you hide your spark, bury your ideas, keep your questions and notions from the team, you have hurt them as badly as if you had stolen a laptop and fenced it on eBay.

A lunch meeting

During my brief career at Yahoo!, I started things. That's my nature; it's the only thing I know how to do.

One day, about three weeks after my arrival, I organized a lunch with a dozen people in other departments so we'd have a chance to connect and brainstorm.

When I got back from lunch, my boss told me that I shouldn't do that anymore. "Cool it," he said, instructing me to just sit in my cube and await instructions.

It's possible that you have a boss like this. If so, I can recommend two things:

1. Ignore this book (for now).

2. Start looking for a new gig, ASAP.

(There's a third plan, one that I'll describe here but that you shouldn't take seriously unless you're impatient, bold, and determined to make a difference: ignore your boss and keep starting things. It works out in the end.)

If your organization refuses to start, is so busy harvesting that they have no interest in planting, perhaps your investment of time and effort is misplaced.

History recorded my boss's tenure at Yahoo! as a failure in the long run. And I was (at least on that day) a failure as an employee for not seeing the world as he did. Failure is an event, though, and with rare exceptions, is not fatal. The process of starting, regularly, and of seeking out opportunities to do it more often, is never a failure. The process is now essential for those who seek to succeed.

When it all falls apart

Vince McMahon started the XFL ten years ago. Football is not a new idea; neither is TV. It took Vince, everyone's favorite crazy showman, to step up and initiate an audacious project built around combining football, TV, and pro wrestling.

A month before the first game, the XFL blimp crash-landed into a restaurant. It was an omen for the entire season. On the coin toss for the first game (sorry, they didn't have a coin toss; they had two guys diving for the football instead), one of the players was injured.

The games were forgettable, the coverage of cheerleaders and other women bordered on misogyny, and the violence was off-putting even to many who loved football. Worse for the league, it was barely covered in the sports pages, and viewership was so low that the other partner, NBC, cancelled coverage after just one year.

A failure by every measure.

Forgive me for being blunt, but "So?"

For all the fear and anxiety and bluffing and stalling and fretting that we devote to starting something, if this is the worst thing that's going to happen to you, it's not so bad.

Vince came out okay. So did NBC. If anything, they both came out ahead compared to those who didn't have the guts to start.

Unless there's a posture within the organization that embraces failure like the XFL, it will be impossible to launch the project that works. It's impossible to have a "success-only" policy. That policy itself will guarantee that there will be no successes.

And if you work for someone with a success-only policy? The choice is whether or not you want to have the same policy, whether you will choose to adopt that as your personal standard for deciding whether or not you initiate.

There will be other jobs, better jobs, bosses more willing to create growth. The only way you will find those jobs and those bosses, though, is to have a personal standard that demands failure, not one that guarantees success. Intellectual integrity goes beyond being clever—it requires that you put your ideas into the world.

"Not what I expected to find"

This is how you know you're hearing the report of a good scientist. Science that comes up with results that surprise the investigator is probably valid, because the self-fulfilling bias hasn't shown up.

Part of initiating is being willing to discover that what you end up with is different from what you set out to accomplish. If you're not willing to discover that surprise, it's no wonder you're afraid to start.

Starting doesn't mean controlling. It means initiating. Managing means controlling, but that's an entirely different skill.

What could you build?

So many doors are open; so much leverage is available. If you could build anything (and you can), what would you build?

- ▷ An institution
- ▷ A religion
- ▷ An idea that spreads
- ▷ A relationship
- ▷ A reputation
- ▷ Cash
- ▷ A practice
- ▷ A job
- ▷ Art
- ▷ Tools
- ▷ A legacy
- ▷ Change that matters

If the only reason you're not initiating a quest for any of these goals is that you're afraid to start, perhaps you ought to think carefully about what's at stake. Have you fully understood the cost of not starting?

Poking Twitter

It's fun to watch a peer start using Facebook or Twitter for the first time. He opens an account, says something fairly inane, and then watches the world poke back.

Wow! I just heard from Lisa... how did she find me so soon?

Hey! I'm tweeting on-board an airplane, and people are tweeting back!

This is an addictive pastime. You take no real risk, touch the world, and it responds. Repeat.

But that's not the starting I'm talking about. It's not a real poke, or real shipping, or real change. It's a zipless version of it, without any opportunity for success or growth.

If you can't fail, it doesn't count.

Initiating is an intentional act

No one answers the phone accidentally. We don't often stumble into a meeting by mistake, or read an e-mail message by chance. Most of what we do at work we do intentionally, with preparation or at least a bit of direct effort.

Starting is like that.

We can schedule for it. Thursday, April 3rd, 3:05... start something.

We can train for it, plan for it, announce it, and even hire for it. If initiating is as essential to the modern organization as it appears, we better be doing all of that and more.

It's not unusual to hear someone say that he is here to help us plan or analyze or review or even fix. We regularly hire people to optimize and synchronize and organize.

So why not invest in starting?

When public school forbids the act of starting

It's not in the curriculum, is it?

How much time do we spend challenging our kids to initiate?

From the high school football team that prohibits the quarterback from calling his own plays, to the jazz band that reads music instead of playing solos, even the extracurricular activities are programmed.

I often encourage kids to start their own clubs, organize their own extracurricular groups. They never do. It's not supposed to be that way, they say.

Is it any wonder we teach this mindset? Factories and managers don't want spunk, or even innovation. They generally seek compliance.

We rely on the disobedient few for innovation, but today, innovation is our only option.

The expensive act of planning on late

When you're late, there's not a lot of room for choice or decision or initiative. When you're late, the path is well lit, and the choices are clear. Run! Run down the path you've run down before.

Late is a tool for people unable to find the guts to stand for their acts. Late gives us cover; it permits us to trample forward, without creativity or panache. "Can't you see I'm late!" we shout, as we do what we have to do, without even pausing to think about what we could do instead.

Late might be useful, except that late is incredibly expensive. This strategy, the one we choose so we can avoid the fear of choice, costs us in so many ways. It degrades quality, misses airplanes, charges overtime, and shuts down those around us. It's also exhausting.

The alternative to planning on late is to initiate before it's required, to ship before deadline, to put the idea out there before the crisis hits. This act of bravery actually gives you influence, leverage, and control in a way that planning on late never can.

Dandelion Mind

In 1998, Cory Doctorow and his wife had a baby girl. Becoming a father led to this insight, which might just change your life:

Mammals invest a lot of energy in keeping track of the disposition of each copy we spawn. It's only natural, of course: we invest so much energy and so many resources in our offspring that it would be a shocking waste if they were to wander away and fall off the balcony or flush themselves down the garbage disposal. We're hardwired, as mammals, to view this kind of misfortune as a moral tragedy, a massive trauma to our psyches so deep that some of us never recover from it.

It follows naturally that we invest a lot of importance in the individual disposition of every copy of our artistic works as well, wringing our hands over "not for resale" advance review copies that show up on Amazon and tugging our beards at the thought of Google making a scan of our books in order to index them for searchers. And while printing a book doesn't take nearly as much out of us as growing a baby, there's no getting around the fact that every copy printed is money spent, and every copy sold without being accounted for is money taken away from us.

There are other organisms with other reproductive strategies. Take the dandelion: a single dandelion may produce 2,000 seeds per year, indiscriminately firing them off into the sky at the slightest breeze, without any care for where the seeds are heading and whether they'll get an hospitable reception when they touch down.

And indeed, most of those thousands of seeds will likely fall on hard, unyielding pavement, there to lie fallow and unconsummated, a failure in the genetic race to survive and copy.

But the disposition of each—or even most—of the seeds [isn't] the important thing, from a dandelion's point of view. The important thing is that every spring, every crack in every pavement is filled with dandelions.

That's the goal, isn't it? For every crack to be filled with your ideas and innovations and creativity? The only way to achieve this, though, is to be prepared for many of them to fail, to land on pavement, to be perfect yet cease to grow.

We can cry about these failures, but that will lead us to hold back on the next idea. Or we can celebrate them, realizing that it's proof that we're being promiscuous in our shipping, putting the best work we can into the world, regardless of whether this particular idea actually works.

When was the last time you set out to be promiscuous in your failures?

Riding a bike and being an adult

I was helping a kid learn how to ride a two-wheeler. He informed me that he didn't really want to learn to ride a bike. His reasons were quite thoughtful: he doesn't live near a bike path, he doesn't really have anywhere to ride, it gets his pants dirty, none of his friends ride bikes, and so on.

Upon engaging in some Socratic dialogue, though, we eventually got to the heart of the matter: he was afraid to learn.

We're extremely adroit at hiding our fear. Most of our lives in public are spent papering over, rationalizing, and otherwise denying our fear. We go to war because we're afraid, and we often go to spiritual events for the very same reason.

We're not kids and this is not a bike.

The purpose of this manifesto is not to magically extinguish your fear. It's to call its bluff. Identifying the "fear of go" is the first step on the road to making the fear go away. If you can embrace the idea that your success and happiness are tied up in defeating the fear that's holding you back, you're 90 percent of the way to where you need to go, because no, we're not kids, and no, this is not a bike.

What to do with good ideas?

Are you one of *those* people?

One of the people with too many good ideas? The folks who have notebooks filled with notions, or daydreams filled with the future?

You've certainly met these people. They're too busy taking notes to get anything done, too busy inventing to actually instigate.

To stop this process, one needs to do only two things:

Start. And then...

Ship.

Can't do the second if you don't do the first.

Paul is one of those people. And he carries the ideas around like a bag of rocks, insulation against criticism, protection from blame. "Hey, can't you see I've got this big notebook full of ideas? Of course you can't hold me responsible for accomplishing anything, I've been too busy thinking up the next thing.... If only those jerks on the Group W bench would listen to me, everything would be fine."

The problem, I think, has nothing to do with the jerks he works for, and everything to do with a fear of starting. His incessant brainstorming also gives him the pleasure of having a great excuse at the same time he's avoiding the short-term pain of failure.

Fear on the left, fear on the right

not enough   too much

Some of us hesitate when we should be starting instead. We hold back, promise to do more research, wait for a better moment, seek out a kinder audience.

This habit is incredibly common. It eats up our genius and destroys our ability to make the contribution we're quite capable of making. Call it *hypogo*—trapped into not enough starting.

Surprisingly, the flip side is also true.

Some people deal with the fear and hide out by doing something else. They overstart, constantly dreaming up the next big thing, bigger than big. They might start a zeppelin transit company on

Monday, and then drop it for a Stirling engine patent application on Wednesday, and perhaps, if that doesn't take off in just a day or two, aim for a business focused on home delivery of notary services by the end of the week.

Fitzgerald nailed it when he described Jay Gatsby's attitude: "What would be the use of doing great things if I could have a better time telling her what I was going to do?" It's easy to fall so in love with the idea of starting that we never actually start.

The person who constantly asks questions, interrupts, takes endless notes, and is always in your face isn't just annoying—she's self-sabotaging, a form of hiding. This *hypergo* mindset is just as safe as the more prevalent kind of under-shipping, because if you're the kind of person who's always dreaming and riffing, of course you can't be held responsible for your work. First, because you're crazy, and second, because you're too busy doing the next thing to be held responsible for the last one.

It's not good to be too fat or too thin. Not good to have blood pressure that's too high or too low. It's only in the center, where we resonate with the market and get it right, that we can produce effectively.

For every person I know who has the hypergo mindset, I know ninety-nine who could contribute by starting more than they do, but don't. If you're not making a difference, it's almost certainly because you're afraid. And that fear might manifest itself at either end of the spectrum.

It doesn't hurt to ask

Actually, it does hurt. It does hurt to ask the wrong way, to ask without preparation, to ask without permission. It hurts because you never get another chance to ask right.

If you run into Elton John at the diner and say, "Hey Elton, will you sing at my daughter's wedding?" it hurts any chance you have to get on Elton John's radar. You've just trained him to say "no"; you've taught him that you're both selfish and unrealistic.

If a prospect walks into your dealership, and you walk up and say, "Please pay me two hundred thousand dollars right now for this Porsche," you might close the sale. But I doubt it. More likely than not, you've just pushed this prospect away, turned the sliver of permission you had into a wall of self-protection.

I got a note last week from a stranger. "I hear you'll be heading to LA," he started, and then invited himself to spend half an hour backstage at a full-day seminar I was doing. I'm confident that he meant well and figured that this is part of what it means to poke the box, to try the new thing. I'm also fairly certain that his lack of preparation and his decision to ask a question where the answer is certainly "no" are just the work of the lizard brain, setting him up to fail, because it's easier than succeeding. What a great excuse for not succeeding—he asked and it got him nowhere!

Every once in a while, of course, asking out of the blue pays off. So what? Even (especially) people who want to initiate need to be smart about priorities and payoffs.

Instead of propositioning everyone within reach of your e-mail box, invest some time and earn the right to ask. Do your homework. Build connections. This makes the risk on your part a lot bigger because you've invested more than two minutes. Initiating when you have more to lose is often better than just winging it.

Buzzer management

The best way to lose at Jeopardy has nothing to do with preparation or smarts. People lose at Jeopardy because they're not good at using the buzzer.

Buzz too early and Alex won't have finished reading the question. Buzz too late and someone else gets to answer it.

And so it goes with go-ing.

We all know the obnoxious co-worker who's too aggressive, too sure it is time to buzz in, too annoying to get anything done.

And in response, we overreact and do too little.

Like most things that matter, starting is an artful choice, not a black and white process. If you're not making the impact you are capable of, perhaps it's time to think harder about how you use the buzzer.

So how? How to get better at this?

My bet is that your current problem is that you don't buzz enough. Most people don't. We hold back. We want to be sure.

Yes, there's the minority that buzzes too often. If it's you, you probably realize it.

The solution seems simple to me. Buzz more. See what happens. Buzz even more. Repeat. As you increase your willingness to buzz in, you'll intersect with the market, with bosses and co-workers and people willing to buy from you. What happens?

Sure, ideas that spread, win, but ideas that don't get spoken always fail.

Fear of hubris

The lesson of Icarus is burned into all of us, even those who can't remember their Greek mythology. The gods get angry at those who would dare to fly, and the penalty is incredibly severe.

In Australia, they call it the "tall poppy" problem. Don't stand up and stand out, or you'll get cut down.

We're trained to fit in, not to stand out, and the easiest way in the world to fit in is to never initiate. Don't speak up. If you see something, don't say anything.

In fact, we spend most of our days waiting for permission to start. And that's why I published this rant.

If you know someone who needs permission, share this with him. If you needed permission, think about the mentor or coach or friend who gave this to you. *Someone is giving you permission.* Someone, perhaps indirectly, hired you, funded you, trained you, encouraged you—all so that you would see something that needed to be done and do it.

It's not hubris. It's essential.

But what if everyone does this? What if everyone speaks up, notices things, starts things, and believes in making a ruckus?

Well, then you'll have a new problem, won't you? You'll have a whole set of new problems, in fact.

You'll have the problem of choosing which great new ideas are worth pursuing and which ones aren't actually so great.

And you'll have the problem of shipping the very best nascent notions out the door.

Both of these are good problems, and neither of them has anything to do with angering the gods or falling out of the sky.

Starting as a way of life

Innovation is mysterious. Inspiration is largely unpredictable. But it's obvious from all the success we see in the marketplace that we can rise to the occasion.

Once the habit is ingrained and you become the starter, the center of the circle, you will find more and more things to notice, to instigate, and to initiate. Momentum builds and you get better at generating it. If you go to bed at night knowing that people are expecting you to initiate things all day the next day, you'll wake up with a list. And as you create a culture of people who are always seeking to connect and improve and poke, the bar gets raised.

What might be considered a board-level decision at one of your competitors' companies gets done as a matter of course. What might be reserved for a manager's intervention gets handled at the customer level, saving you time and money (and generating customer joy).

This incredibly prosaic idea, the very simple act of initiating, is actually profoundly transformative.

Forward motion is a defensible business asset.

Safe

Halloween is not safe. Something bad might happen. In fact, sooner or later, it probably will.

Flying is not safe. You and I both know a dozen or a hundred or a thousand ways an angry person can wreak havoc.

Selling is not safe. You might (in fact you will) be rejected.

Golf is not safe. My grandfather died playing golf.

Speaking up is not safe. People might be offended.

Innovation is not safe. You'll fail. Perhaps badly.

Now that we've got that out of the way, what are you going to do about it? Hide? Crouch in a corner and work as hard as you can to fit in?

That's not safe, either.

Might as well do something that matters instead.

GO GO GO

If you get in the habit of shipping things, of making a difference and of poking the box, that's your doing, and the rest of us will take pleasure in enjoying the fruits of your bravery.

If you don't start, if you pull back into your shell, if you recoil in fear at this extraordinary opportunity (and obligation), then blame me. I clearly didn't do a good enough job of cajoling and daring you into doing the work you're capable of, the work that matters.

You can't lose.

Go.

"There are two mistakes one can make
along the road to truth.

Not going all the way, and not starting."

Siddhārtha Gautama

Acknowledgments

Thanks to Dan Slater for poking the box. To Ishita Gupta, Lisa DiMona, Lisa Gansky, Jacqueline Novogratz, Vicky Griffith, Russ Grandinetti, Sarah Tomashek, Terry Goodman, and Jeff Bezos for egging me on. Always bonus thanks to Catherine E. Oliver and Red Maxwell. To Helene, Alex & Mo. And thanks to the smart and talented publishing community that supports authors and their ideas—giants like Adrian Zackheim, Michael Cader, Stuart Krichevsky, Pam Dorman, Wendy Bronfin, Megan Casey, independent booksellers, and anyone who ever paid money for a book. Paul Robinson, Martha Cleary, Corey Brown, Gil to the Rescue, and Jonathan Hull helped with the tech. Kudos to the authors who are at the top of their game, giving far more than they get, including Neil Gaiman, Kevin Kelly, Susan Piver, Pema Chodron, Zig Ziglar, Tom Peters, Max Barry, Cory Doctorow, Steve Pressfield, Kurt Andersen, and Elizabeth Gilbert. Thanks to boingboingers Mark Frauenfelder and Xeni Jardin for poking every day, and to anyone who has a blog and lives to provoke, in a good way.

This book is dedicated in memory of my mom. People who knew her will understand.

About The Domino Project

Books worth buying are books worth sharing. We hope you'll find someone to give this copy to. You can find more about what we're up to at http://www.TheDominoProject.com

Here are three ways you can spread the ideas in this manifesto:

1. Hold a discussion group in your office. Get people to read the book and come in and argue about it. How open is your company to innovation and failure? What will you do if your competitors get better at it than you are?

2. Give away copies. Lots of them. It turns out that when everyone in a group reads the same thing, conversations go differently.

3. Write the names of some of your peers on the inside back cover of this book (or scrawl them on a Post-it on your Kindle). As each person reads the book, have them scratch off their name and add someone else's.

We hope you'll share.

About the cover

The man in a hurry is an archetype, first discovered in the hieroglyphs of ancient Egypt. He's you, the excited, optimistic experimenter who understands that risk is misunderstood and that forward motion is the key to success. The image is a trademark of The Domino Project, but you have our permission to use it non-commercially, to encourage your peers to go.

Thanks for reading.